Psalm

Psalm

Poems by Carol Ann Davis

T|P

Tupelo Press
Dorset, Vermont

COPYRIGHT

Contents

for my father,
James Russell Davis
February 18, 1930–September 7, 2001

Stars I think about, if I could fly, I could reach in a few old-fashioned days. But physicists' stars I use as buttons, buttoning up curtains of emptiness. If I stretch my arms next to the rest of myself and wonder where my fingers are—that is all the space I need.

—Willem de Kooning

INVOCATION INSIDE A LINE BY OROZCO

Come this small morning,
I want you to, the dawn not yet here,
tell me the secret of the doves,
not yet awake, the typewriter keys
misspent, my mind misspent,

                                       your sightings
having come in sleep and dropped away, stones,
the first and the last, thought-shadows and the nothing that follows:
grace of what is
                         would you like me to begin inside that?

Try again? The corn maze with a secret
at its heart, something about the county fair
on the radio because
                         it's getting colder as you liked—

the dawn this purple color

and cooler now, the grasses bent
and brown. You would be awake at this hour,

at this hour you would be at the kitchen sink,
above as below. Instead the story

of *playing Vivaldi to fifty gorillas* in the camps, music
for the end of the world, something like that, the world

of your boyhood. I know nothing about it. Inside me
it becomes air,
                  blue then purple, then fully light, everyone

sleeping deeper without this restlessness. What would I tell you,
what would you want to know of me? Nothing

or you'd have come sooner, sent a child, sent an animal
with a note at its collar:

> I don't want to tell you more gossip
> because you've been
> *letting it slip*—

when I see you next, we'll both be so much river marsh,
nothing in current

we can hear or say.

SMALL BOY

How does he keep his hand to his heart,
the other to the olive sprig,
600 years with his back to Memling's cracked gold,
and if this is a wall, what wall,
where? If a wall, then a square nearby,
worn blue stones, and old men telling fortunes
no one pays them for.
                    Memling's given the boy wings
outlined in pigeon gray, and a boy's tunic,
a boy's pursed mouth, eyes that reflect
the same light the olives catch. Maybe the light's
the church door opened to noon, the square asleep
as if poached in oil. Or it's the square of a window
in a monk's cell, quick daylight where no monk has slept in years,
but somehow, one last question of faith
moistens the air
                    until it is no longer a small matter.

Where someone thought to cross the river,
a medieval bridge is standing,
its millstone long since rolled into the riverbed
and become native. Just inside the church,
someone whitewashed a wall, painted it with gilt,
the blue of a boy's tunic not so blue
as his shadow, if he can still cast one. Not so blue
as the vein he means you to see, yours
under his skin.

Listening to Willem Squeal while a Selmer Guitar Reminds Me of the Existence of All Things

In the psalms, it's all right to want,
it's all right to starve,
to pledge yourself to the air—

and the three leaves we picked up
off the trail last week
deepen into a red

they halfway wanted. Guitar strains
stretch from the state border
into the Atlantic

with its cliff and shelf, the window's blind blades
meaning something just now,
behind them, the sick crepe myrtle,

ghost of a maple. Love is round,
is perseverance, is next week
paid in horsehair. Love owns

this part of the melody, turns the world
away from ruin for the second it takes
to inhale a breath,

then for less than that,
obscures the chords
so I hear my own ear canal contract,

and the melody again,
translucent under the skin.
In this muddy room,

a measure's left to keep proving
it still wants us,
our world quickly made

of stones and river water
and grief transmuted into fire.

Distal

As I walk along St. Philips, dusk fills my lungs
and the bells of six o'clock make equations
in the air. On my corner
the lights set the church on fire,
the houses surround in a kind of kneel.

Where's Fra Angelico now? I've wanted to lick
his frescoes and taste watercolor ribs.
I've wanted to eat off Flow Blue
before machines made lines precise enough

the ceramic no longer gave. If I'm still,
things around me move back in their tracks,
but not far enough. It will be hard to see it

when my own heart
drops into my hand like a fish.
It will be hard to be done seeing.

View of Delft

The human figures
seem to match in vacancy
the waiting boat,
its scrubbed planks and face.

Like an afterthought, the water
cuts through the picture below-meridian,
shines at a slant like a knife on a cutting board—

               from this view,
one can guess how the customs house door
arches into total darkness, which is to say
fine buildings are reflected
in the brown water, nothing more
than a shallow swath
catching imaginary light
from the sky;

               the city floats
between this water
and insubstantial heaven,
the water, between blue shingles of castle
and two nuns—
one thin, one round—
their habits set
against the weight
and business of the wharf,
they must think:
what we are God is not.
Detail on the steeples.
God is not. Perfect angles.

Grief Daybook I

It's the third hour
in this clear light,

a thing covered
in seconds,

pacing the long apparatus
of a thought

and leaving twigs,
orange juice, on the table

papers still heavy
with requests.

This morning I want to drive the six hours home
just to touch the stone

over my father's heart,
his name chiseled into vowels

and consonants. I want to camp there,
to sleep there

where other mourners
come looking for someone else

and cross over us. What is the heart
but a request? What is it

to be long dead, dead a week,

a year? For a second,
I am a riverbed, my one eye

dusty with watching the blue above.
The visitors to my grave

are heavy to hold up, the earth
dissolute, a solution of sugars

and branches' marrow.

Out of Sixteen Portraits, One Turns to Look

—for Anna Akhmatova

Prison gates at this hour
smell of sulfur and burn the tongue.

•

On the third day she gets up and makes tea.

•

As if there is something besides river to be found,
the ice breaks up.

•

A bird caught in thistle,
thistle caught in water.

•

Asia, Abyssinia, the Crimea, we are tired.

•

Sensei, all long train rides lead into a square.

•

The boulevards just swept and finished,
the paint tasting of wax and powders.

•

The Futurists and Acmeists can leave me for dead for all I care.

•

And with "just the right figure for ballet."

•

At this hour the window she's chosen
to be her son's eye is a blank stone among stones,

•

her face to him a white impression on snow.

•

And gunshots and the shops always dark;
a forest of suicides from factories that smell of candy.

•

I take it all back, how it seemed, how it was.

•

The river over reason is at war with sky.

•

Clock on the dresser, half-drunk glass.

A Hundred Wild Geese

Each curved neck
          wants me to learn more about geometry,

telemetry, reeds.
          On this scroll, pill-bodies suspend

in the snowy sky, Ma Fen's monochrome.
          It's before the new style

to compose "everything in one corner,"
          so the field is busy

with all manner of movement;
          some fish the white lake—

the line of its surface a glance at order—
          others land

or practice landing as if haunted by the freak storm
          that led them there.

Above them,
          near-suicides arrow earthward,

their black wings solid as metal,
          sculpted in midair to fix ruin,

a flood, the death of a son.

          Sometimes the land is too white to find,

these little geese given the shape
          of what is holy, what flown.

I Wanted It So

It was winter.
It was winter and the paper wanted dove-fingers.
It was winter so the pond grew a blind eye.
It was winter—so clear air, so water just burned.
I could hear your lungs
distilling the air, unhinging choice January days
to console you later. Because you thought
that would be part of going away. Winter was a pet stone
in our pet mouths. Winter was no one sitting
in our sitting room. Though we searched,
we found no friends handy. Our own reflections
grew to suit us. And the winter light
I meant to keep you inside.

The Death of the Age of Reason

Because I am equal parts salt and dust
solutions are hard to come by. All things

have their fulfillment
because the horizon is straight

then round. Because we look back
we are given what was probable

and not the thing that was.
Because I did not keep it well

it prefigures itself. Because I did not think
of gravesites

they grew wings. He ate and slept
and counted our years on his hands

because he was a man—
sat in chairs, hated fish,

folded our clothes because, because.
It happened just this way,

didn't it? A square window,
ordinary sky. Nurses passing

in the halls, the still
of tide shift

and two o'clock. His son recounting
the events of his life aloud.

Because I worried over you
you were taken from me.

PLAINSONG

And the dogs will have their routes,
the birds will be uncovered breathing
in the trees, the delivery boys

will hold their fancy books of orders. Coming in low
in fog, the Remembrance Day bombers

fly their rotations, the ocean grown senile,
the intersections safe
in their half-drawn Xs

—Love's Car Service
and the boys outside it
smoking.

In the Room

Where real air hurries into schools
to lick the claws of mangroves,

he wakes
from something very near
time beginning again,

my father's breath startled, as if
it all could come back to him at once.

Outside, freeway and river
seem to balance out.

He doesn't squeeze my hand
so much as worry
a familiar spot deep in my palm,

an old habit
just turned up in him,
one that signals
I'm awake because
he can't make a sound,

and if I'm lucky I look over
in time to see the underbelly of one blue eye

find its spot below the lid
where an imprint of the window
nearing orange

like the sun burned into the eye
must be.

CENOTAPH

After the so-much-work of fireflies,
they come from town to ring the bell.
Somewhere a stone is laid over. Like them,
I've held the closed corpses of Romans
to my ear like a loved thing. When they come,
my shoulders are covered with blue cloth,
the bell hung just as they left it. For feast day,
the boy-miracle is stored in the silo. In my cell,
a tiny dream of olives has gone looking for deep water
without my help. The day is coming
—as on the fresco in the church—
when I'll spring out of Adam's torso half-formed.
I'll not know whose blessing to want.
I'll walk up to Jesus and take his terra cotta hand
as if it would part from his body to be mine.
Where angels and devils are carving worlds out of fruit,
I'll discover I've been given no eyes or ears or mouth.
No one will tell me not to eat
the bit of original wood
in my hand.

Winter Mix

This is a day with ghosts in it,
with husks and some kind of confession

at its heart. I'm not up to it, fazed from memory
and a light sleep, from stray cats and mice.

One day I won't wake up to my father's portrait.
I'll take it and put it
in the sitting room
and it will become small to me,

but that day is years off
and full of its own fevers.
For now, his boy's eyes
make me into something,

into cumulus and cirrus,
into ganglia and spine,
into zephyrs and waves. I'm sorry
to come with empty hands.

Catalogos

Inside the mustard seed's halo:
a dream of birds. On the tongue
of the samurai: a sugary
oath. On the lens of the architekton:
a history of the Russian Revolution.
In the ear of the rosebud:
continuous time. Above the fur of the newt:
hapless flea-eyes. On the tip
of recorded geology: a Rome apple.
Inside the eye of the loon:
high tea. In the far corner
of the second-floor broom closet:
jumper cables, an earring. In the wheel-well
of the container ship:
a dog named Drew.
On the cobalt mind
of the window-dressing:
love's appetite, genesis. Atop the jawed terrain
of the Azores: rumor-prone Titanium.
On the tongue of the Pallid Bat:
blue oregano, the dream
of a visit to Dresden. Within
the gone byways of thought-patterns:
a vial of Opium. In the marsh-mud,
favored habitat of the Standard Nightjar:
a groom's stable with a horse
called Lucky Lady. In the book
predicting the birth of the prophet-boy:
the short spelling of sloe-eyed.
In the long canal of a swimmer's ear:
the carp's lovely evolution,
its given-up-for-dead
atlas of the world.

GRIEF DAYBOOK II

There are panels of sky
as good as forgotten,
Evans' gelatin folds of Florida
circa 1934. The line of sky is dark at first

where the gulf lifts it,
then comes to me like a halo
around the palm tree with its neck bent,

its spray of branches
leaning out of frame
as if to flee. Its roots pull
at sand, as if to say,
this is what it takes.
I'd believe, if not for the way

my breath catches,
if not for the wild faint
sleep's become. The palm's branches

are spears left
where they've fallen
in the dirty sand, too heavy

for the tide to take them. Where the neck bends,
cut branches—like stubble on a chin
as seen from below—seem to ask

something of the photographer,
something not washed away

in the chemical bath. The shadow of the trunk
just underlines—means to prove the existence
of the world. It's three o'clock

and the latticework of 1934
is pulling around me in this light

as if to say *my god, my god,*
a hymn sung
by infidels to believers
as a way to ask for water.

Willem at Four Months with Matisse in Morocco

You're afraid of mirrors.
When nothing consoles,
what you find in the sea-blue
just beyond a girl's dark hair
sets your mouth a little open, quiet.

No interest yet in the veil,
in the orange fish, three of them,
their yellow undercoats swimming.
Your own fish-eye is incomprehensible.

Behind them, a night-blue wall makes everything real,
background to your first dreams. If she floats
among so many blues much longer,
she might stop being something else,

become a girl posed
with her legs crossed under her.
She kneels our way
about to make the best tea,

her slippers off; if she said something,
it would be one natural word,
something she learned at your age.

Her robe's yellow pattern mutes
to green diamonds near her face,
an ellipsis of flesh with a full mouth,
stick-eyes you'll know one day without asking why.

There's a window somewhere
giving a triangle of light,
imperfect for being early,
the very early morning

of tea not yet made, slippers off,
as I said before—there's something

one's sadness allows;
blues you find
as if born to them.

ELEGY ON HORSEBACK IN THE CAMARGUE

I can still see the half-wild horse I rode
through the marsh, the backs of the horses

he followed. When he jumped a stream
with you six weeks inside me,

I didn't think of life being made of nothing sturdy,
cells on the uterine wall

nearly undoing grief into hoofprint. I thought
no such thing, just that I was far away

from everything, having just learned
the word *roan* in French, having just seen

the Black Madonna in the cellar
below the church. When unsaddled horses

came upon us on the trail, our own
newly small and tame, maybe it was your sleeping

(as now, but then inside me)
that slowed their advance,

sent their backs twitching into tall grass,
let them let us go.

THE BURNISHED THING

Inside the little box: a burnished thing,
a glass egg, but what's at its center?
And what are we to do
with our knowledge of it? Say I'm sorry,
the world meant you no harm,
then swarmed you again
and now we don't know
if you're animal or mineral?
This began inside Cornell's mind,
burned in the oven for age,
a series of twigs and branches
disarranged to suggest
the sky above a field of lavender—
like so many, he was partial to girls
lunching at automats, a certain age.

Does this help one with the bombings? The torture,
the light in the Xstrasse
the day after the Anschluss,
Gerti on her train to Geneva? Life
is funny. So are facts,
lined up and elemental
inside the language, a pictograph
unrolled in yellow and blue,
so many rivers to be traced,
loved first as syllables. My burned thing
becomes me. See it there?
It won't stop wanting us
no matter what we do to it.

Ars Poetica inside an Evans Photograph

Because the book is still open,
the girl with the light eyes

stares at me, not
into the canyon

of her brother's brow
on the facing page—

she holds up the round head
and ellipsis of hat,

hair the color of straw,
straw the color of sun, such that

shadows become black rings
at the photographer's feet. On the underlip,

ink, interruption, a word memorized
then called away. Nearby, boots

line a shelf, calendars reading
June-July-August,

the days no more consumed
than overgrown. Before long,

thoughts catch in the verticals
of the house's wood slats,

in the dust we are born to. Set to meet all
coming and going, the rims

of her coronas arc up
toward fine eyelashes. Just up ahead,

there's a rumor of rainfall
it's a test to disbelieve.

The Stave Church Paintings, Norway

On the wood a wide-eyed saint
of travellers or of the cold,
a red halo drawn as if with crayon,
and a black outline

to show where halo ends
and North Sea moves out
past horizon. Underneath
the grain cracks almost in harmony
with the narrative. At his waist,

bench meets sea in a perfect horizontal,
and above, a focal point in the blue
knots where the saint wills something

to happen. Where the paint is worn through
something has escaped,
as it must, the saint's skin
white as pine. On cold nights here

the wood was prepared,
chalk ground into its flaws
then sealed, then covered in linen
like a corpse, and left to dry

in a church
where herders came in
to pray, to keep warm,

the painting taking shape and with it
the winter, each morning
something new on the wall:

background color,
the hint of a skull, an ankle
thin as a child's. The saint's aspect
unfixed there for days,

newborn, disoriented save
the smell of wool.

CHAOS THEORY

Let the boy slip by the wire unharmed.

Let the lost gloves convene in the square, a blizzard.

Let the ocean turn heathen.

Let the starlings bypass the campanile.

Let the agnostics sleep through the night.

Let the Baedeker redraw the borders.

Let the Church of John Coltrane break at noon for cookies and punch.

Let all teleologies lead to long naps. No fingerpainting, no modern dance.

Let the fugue out of its tiny room.

Let the infanta rue the discussion.

Let the American grizzly lead.

Let phenomenology drive for once!

Let the pieta vanish into salt water.

Let the submariners up.

Let the groom out of the stable. And the paints.

Let the novitiate have the chocolate brioche.

What the Poem Wants

I am wanting everything from the poem right now.
I'm wanting years I wasn't born,
my father a young man on a street he's memorized
in the hottest part of the day.
Going to a diner he knows. Or a movie.
The poem covers that over,
pulls the sheet over its head without my asking.
It happens all the time. It all does.
The poem is stealing from Plenty Coups, the great warrior,
his secret recipe for jerked beef. And from the air,
the idea that language puts the coin between our teeth.
Let me wander inside that, I ask the poem,
and come back saved.
But not now. I'm three floors up;
the footsteps and engine exhaust rise and fill my room,
and I'm becoming a beggar, or beggar lice, or moths–
I'm spilled everywhere. The thief in me
would sleep off these hours, their gravel
and jackals and graves, none of them real,
but the poem is not partial to waste.
The child in me donates my fingers to the poem,
would cut them off and use them in soup
if that would bring the poem happiness
or even rest. But the poem is ashamed I feel that way,
sorry for my teeth, and fingers,
and the eyes in my head.
Never mind, the poem says. It was nothing.

THE NEXT TIME

you come here, certain of nothing, not sure
                                    what a name is

or what it's for, remember the boy you saw
                        climbing the palm

to get at its heart, how he threw the knife into the sand
                                    at his sister's feet,

then jumped back into the day
                        of the church parking lot. Remember the MedU,

their generators so much leftover ocean sound, and the bells
                                    which told the time

too often. Recall without regret
                        the Laffy-Taffy Charlie gave your son

each time you bought eggs and how later he could say
                                    "own bag" and "thanks"

and open the door himself. Benignly occlude
                        the fire station

with its two open eyes, among so many wooden houses
                                    its siren regular. The next time

regret nothing. Notice nothing that doesn't lead to your own absolution;
                                    absolve nothing

that eats or ignores or steals, but save room

                              for Manchu's sweet whine,

your son's way of naming things something else

                              even before they brought him

out of you

          into the world.

Columbarium

—for Bruno Schulz and Joseph Cornell

Little drawer with things in it   breath of a saint
the tower and the wheel   sleeve of a dress
the night sky with a hinge attached   Mayakovsky on the Trans-Siberian
with a girl named Jude   phenomenon of the canteen
the penny arcade glistening with light just now   or knowledge

train schedules fluttering to small destinies   the town asleep
the shtetl razed   where did we live before this?   animate the elms,
the birches on my cue   all down the parkway
such a thing existing   the boy counting to ten inside the Palestrina
the tackle box alight with horsehair flies   lost strings of rivers
maps of gone places   (Lvov)

Bruno the teacher of drafting with the fetish for feet   not so unusual
but gone now   for other reasons   his pencil-drawn tailor's dummies
posed   girls really   the other (Joseph) bicycling along the Promenade
thoughts of Medici   feeling of skyline   the bridge a cathedral
or nearly   in this fog

Lucky goes green   give me your manifesto   I need a cushion
a ballerina for my scrapbook   the annunciation as fresco-bait
churches gone dark with the human figure   dovecotes
the young dancer asleep in leotard   swans in open air, St. Petersburg
stray wings   promise of electricity
feeling of skywardness   mussed-up feeling

so many historic crossings   Picasso from Barcelona to the pink period
the lungs of the ship   and the French primer   a few key words
the writing brush comes forward and says   *daba-daba-daba-daba*
Takuan with an ink brush on his carpet   a day not unlike this one
ten watch faces strung alongside the white parrot cut-out
who would keep me   the parrot asks

Lorca's deep song   dynasty of persimmons   and a hundred small ways
of keeping alive   blue ceilings repel wasps and fascinate birds
the trinity forbids us walking under ladders   but still of an evening
with so many facades   be ready with the snow   the small flood
the room stripped to elements,   to bellcast
pencil drawing abloom   with mongrel-smoke

his street corner dusty at noon   both of them gone, Bruno first, then Joseph
the bridge always half-flown   the still photos   analogy preserving the blind in us
from whence the idea arose for bedtime   for mercy among the drowned *Right now,*
do you have a phrase that goes beyond the barrier?   Takuan again, mumbling

the one taken   the one called back   certainty of ideas
alight in wind   the bed was here   the desk, the window
and what passes   among starling-notes

ALL SOULS'

The dead's ashy faces grow ashier
for their not being around, I know,
but not yet, not now.

I like how it is
when the day rolls over
and nothing's on its back. Nothing

like a complaint crossing the sky,
a freight whistle coming along
like it means what's promised. This is how

the world turns good,
over and over again, the butcher up early,
the bird's half-wing

glossy where it fell,
creation turned bare as a seed. In my bare feet
I'm walking the floor,

the wood grain mysterious
for my attentions. In this way
my ancient dream of the dustbowl

is fulfilled, its ear of periwinkle,
blue field of wheat.

NAMING YOU

—for my son Willem

Before you were named, you came in a white boat.
It was the first of many crossings
in which grief held a sprig

of olive. It was a day with blind heat
and no small number of finches. I mean to record
that in Siena the lily had grown imperceptible
on the church wall, rubbed to nothing

by believers in mortar, in paint. I considered Indigo,
its long history, then ate some Chinese
which made me sick. Like licking a stamp
to the nether world

or pasting illustrations to a letter
by way of worship. Before you were named

I had a name for a little while, not long. It was Dispirito
and went back after a week to its native land. Before that,
Queens was Queens and the automats were filled
with girls from Macy's,

but most of that world is gone now,
my little map of sky, my archivist of bone.
Now the 100 names for god
build a pile of sticks at your feet, if you have feet.

If you have eyes you know about
the paucity of still rooms. If you like

you can run into the yard
when you hear the train coming.

For Johns in South Carolina

I'm no longer tired, no longer small
when I look down
on the suggestion of diving board,
maybe Johns' own feet below me,
and arrows to show that the hands
stop mid-section,
then arc out to disappear
along that invisible curve
into a dark water of paint.

The gradient of the wall behind
comes through the paper, makes a counter-pattern
but not really; there's no story here,
nothing to see but whites rising up
away from plate-glass blue.

Did he paint this
out at Edisto, no such blue there,
Frank O'Hara's foot-cast
awaiting its wooden box? O'Hara's words
just posted, not yet arrived—
When I think of you in South Carolina
I think of my foot in the sand—

So much lost, ten or twelve layers
of charcoal over pastel,
even what the painting tries to give me now
in black and blue, asking several times
are you up for this? Some energy
one suspects one doesn't have,

the spring-loaded board ready below
with its single trick. Outside, a cloud passes over
and darkens this page, as when a neighbor stops on my porch
to look in the window box,
thinking no one home.

Feast Day Elegy

Here is the feast day with its large hands
and mouth, its river sound and clay color,
the town concerned just now with bathing

and gathering wood. I won't be here again,
this year of 3,000 days
closing its fist to me lovingly as it must,

its five fingers and veins and nail
turned to no sound, no voice. I want,
as Thomas did, to say

let us all go to die with him,
but I am passing through
the Middle Ages—I am barely seeing
crosses hammered into simple squares.

When the future comes, it will empty of me, too,
and the saint that comforted me
will empty into gilt shadow.

For now, the garden door
is made of birds, my saint flutters
like a wasp, and the girl's hands
in the painting almost rest in her work

of making thread. She doesn't look at us.
She looks into the paint
where she was made. For her,

the future is a single chair, a pincushion, a bit
of sailor's cloth. The wall behind her

will remain a sky color, the blue
of rocks. And her father will always be
just out of the room, on the point

of calling her name.

Grief Daybook III

Today it's like water in the ear, a slow bleed in the brain,
thinking of your bones
and the marrow inside them. Last night,

half-awake, I leaned into the siren as it passed
and thought of Coltrane writing his liner-note prayer
—*it all has to do with it*—

and listened for the drumbeat of another pulse in me.
It's there, but I can't hear it. In the morning
there will be sunlight and organ music
from the church across the street.

Where you've gone, there will be a night sky of psalms—
a cello's goose neck, fingers waiting
above a stalled note.
                        Oh, ear of my ear,
there's hardly anything
left of you now.

An Understanding between Living and Dead

Come burn my fingers
                    like a little ice age,

unlock the riddle of the Norse,
                            tell me why

and how. Are your veins still blue?
                            Do atmospheres

protect us or not? I'm not air, not sediment,

but animal.
                Here everything slides

into mercury, everything burns
                            at its edge.

Have you seen me among wolves and gnats?

At low tide
            among sand crab?

Or, better,
            after cataclysms,

after rain, so much still hidden?

                            Come for me next.
I will find the train station,
                    and wait there.

Corn Maze Afternoon

There where the blooms of burnt trees are promised. There

where the wet fall begins to yellow, the briskness of the afternoon

leading everyone past the old bobcat

to where the gray wolves circle above a highway.

There where goats nap.

So much to see, and the petting, nearly endless petting,

and so the bettering of habitat. Where the burnt trees gather

beneath orchard signs—"Just Us Orchards"; "Fruitlands"—

a white-eyed dog follows alongside the careless sweep

of your hand. Like skipping a stone. Nothing but grass and the three of us

adrift in the orchard. Much as we will be

long after the defunct mariachi band. Much as we will remain

after heroin park and the noodle house,

our voices echoing in a pool of floating ghosts, of chlorine

—all of it there, waiting for us, our future tied with a knot.

What are the other virtues, the ones after forgetfulness

and praise? And what follows

to resurrect these strewn, strawmade goods?

The last Early Girl glistening on the vine, the ridgeline

awash in light. Here where we climb,

follow signs and answer questions: if Jonah was swallowed

by a whale, turn right, turn right into the corn's

open heart, its many hands.

Acknowledgments

I am grateful for the help of many people, only a few of whom I will mention here: first, for my mother and father, whose early example of reading, writing, and faith never leaves me. Second, for my brothers and sister, whose constancy remains my true north. For Nancy Willard and Frank Bergon, who showed me the possibility of a writing life. For Dara Wier, James Tate, and August Kleinzahler, who showed me its shape. For Garrett and Willem Doherty, who've shown me everything else.

An incalculable debt is owed by all lovers of poetry to Jeffrey Levine and Margaret Donovan, who so sustain it.

Grateful acknowledgment is made to Vassar College and its W. K. Rose Fellowship, which allowed me time to begin these poems. I also thank the editors of those publications in which the following poems originally appeared:

Agni: "Columbarium"
Another Chicago Magazine: "I Wanted It So"
Dislocate: "Chaos Theory"
The Gettysburg Review: "In the Room"
Image: "Grief Daybook II"; "Grief Daybook III"
Indiana Review: "Plainsong"
The Iowa Review: "Out of Sixteen Portraits, One Turns to Look"
Mid-American Review: "Cenotaph"
North American Review: "Listening to Willem Squeal while a Selmer Guitar Reminds Me of the Existence of All Things"
Poetry: "Ars Poetica inside an Evans Photograph"
Prairie Schooner: "What the Poem Wants"; "Small Boy"
The Southern Review: "A Hundred Wild Geese"; "Feast Day Elegy"; "Grief Daybook I"; "Distal" (reprinted in *Best New Poets 2005*)
The Threepenny Review: "For Johns in South Carolina"
TWENTY: South Carolina Poetry Fellows (Hub City, 2005): "Naming You"